FACING IRS PROBLEMS?

Unlock Tax Resolution Strategies for Individuals and Businesses

David B. Greene, Esq.

Jacobs & Whitehall
9600 Escarpment Blvd
Suite 745-282
Austin, TX 78749
www.jacobsandwhitehall.com

Ordering Information:

Quantity sales. Special discounts are available on quantity purchases by corporations, associations, and others. For details, contact the publisher at the address above.

Orders by U.S. trade bookstores and wholesalers. Please contact Jacobs & Whitehall: Tel: (888) 570-7338 or visit www.jacobsandwhitehall.com.

Printed in the United States of America

Published in 2023

ISBN: 978-1-954506-92-3

PREFACE

Have you ever had an IRS agent knock on your door or have you ever received an IRS letter stating that they are going to levy your wages or bank account? If so, you know what fear is. Everyone fears the IRS, even if you have never cheated on your taxes or forgot to file a tax return. After all, it was IRS agents who have brought down many well-known figures.

However, unless you are, in fact, cheating on your taxes and filing fraudulent returns, you do not need to be unduly afraid of the IRS. In this book, I will give you methods of dealing with the revenue officers assigned to collect from delinquent taxpayers and non-filers. Not paying your taxes is not itself a crime, it is a debt to the government. I will introduce you to several ways to deal with that debt and resolve it in a manner that will not unduly burden you.

Almost everyone has, at one time or another, owed back taxes to the government, so don't feel alone if you have that problem. Instead, read on and let this book help you resolve your tax problems and get your life back.

DEDICATION

This book is lovingly dedicated to my parents, who always inspired me to excel, and my wife and daughter, who have always been there to help me through good times and bad.

DISCLAIMER

This publication is intended to be used for educational purposes only. No legal advice is being given, and no attorney-client relationship is intended to be created by reading this material. The author assumes no liability for any errors or omissions or for how this book or its contents are used or interpreted, or for any consequences resulting directly or indirectly from the use of this book. For legal or any other advice, please consult an experienced attorney or the appropriate expert, who is aware of the specific facts of your case and is knowledgeable in the law in your jurisdiction.

Greene Law Firm PA
11 McGee Street
Greenville, SC 29601
(864) 271-7940
www.davidgreeneattorney.com

TESTIMONIALS

"Good morning Mr. Greene. Thank you so much for your help in resolving my Federal and State tax issues. You were highly recommended by others and those recommendations were confirmed with my association with you. Again thank you for all your support and assistance to me in this very stressful ordeal for me."

– S.H.

****

"Wonderful group of professionals, confident & knowledgeable. Use them for all my tax needs (personal/business) & estate planning. Can't say enough about how well this firm takes care of me. They are very kind & personable."

– Rhonda P.

****

"Mr. Greene handled my IRS case with tenacity, professionalism, and efficiency. He is very knowledgeable about these cases and strives to get the best results for the client in terms of a solution. I recommend this firm to anyone who has IRS problems to tackle. I appreciate his efforts and his drive to arrive at a plausible solution."

– A.G.

****

TABLE OF CONTENTS

About The Author

David grew up in Greenville, South Carolina, and has seen this city grow exponentially. He is very proud to call Greenville his home. He is the founder of the Greene Law Firm and has been practicing law for over 46 years. He graduated from Clemson University with a B.S. in physics and continued that discipline at Florida State University where he earned his M. S. and Ph. D. degrees in Experimental Molecular Physics. He then obtained his J. D. degree in law, also from FSU, and was admitted to the South Carolina Bar in 1977.

In 1984 David opened his own practice and, since 1995, has specialized in the Tax Problem Resolution field. David's extensive knowledge of mathematics helps him give his clients a distinct advantage in resolving their IRS problems. At the end of the day, his passion and what excites him is seeing his clients happy with the solution that has been obtained for them and knowing they are "getting their life back."

The IRS Problem Resolution practice provided a natural progression into the field of Estate Planning because he learned that so many people do not know how to preserve and organize their assets for their spouses, children, and other loved ones. He has helped many clients form Trusts and other Estate Planning documents that assure that their assets are protected and are passed to their heirs in the manner they wish.

He is a member of the Greenville County Bar, The South Carolina Bar, the American Association for Justice, and the South Carolina Association for Justice. He is also a member of a national tax problem resolution group, the American Society of Tax Problem Solvers. He is admitted to practice before all South Carolina Courts, the Federal Courts, and the U. S. Tax Court.

Outside of the office, you can usually find David at the family home in Taylors where he and his family enjoy spending time with their German Shepherd and two dachshunds. When he has time, David's other hobby is photography and videography. In the fall David's favorite thing is to attend or watch Clemson football.

David and his family are active members of Scenic Hills Baptist Church.

CHAPTER 1

INTRODUCTION TO THE GREENE LAW FIRM, P.A. IN SOUTH CAROLINA

With over 35 years of experience, our practice provides top-notch tax resolution services to handle various tax problems, from audits to criminal cases, and even incorrect W-2s. Our expertise extends to taxpayers who owe anywhere from $10,000 to a million dollars to the IRS, and non-filers who require their tax returns filed.

What Will Readers Gain From This Book?

Our book is meant to offer readers a sense of peace and assurance that their tax problems can be resolved - and that it's merely a matter of finding the right pathway to do so. We want to reassure our clients that 99% of cases are not criminal, and owing a debt does not lead to imprisonment, as protected by the Constitution. Fraud or expected fraud are the only cases that lead to criminal activity.

We believe that a proactive approach is the best way to resolve tax problems. Through this book, we hope that readers will gain valuable insights into the tax resolution process and learn how to navigate it effectively.

CHAPTER 2

IRS TAX DEBT IN THE UNITED STATES

The Prevalence Of IRS Tax Debt For Americans

The issue of IRS tax debt for Americans has escalated in recent years, particularly due to the COVID-19 pandemic. Many individuals experienced job losses and financial instability, leading to non-payment of taxes. Businesses also faced challenges, contributing to a multi-million-dollar problem for the IRS and the country. The IRS has hired numerous new employees to address the issue, but inadequate training has sometimes exacerbated the problem.

Factors Behind The IRS's Struggles

There are two main reasons for the IRS's current challenges:

1. Pre-pandemic directives: Even before COVID-19, the government and the president instructed the IRS to hire more agents and address tax issues more efficiently.
2. COVID-19 closures: The IRS closed its offices for seven months in 2020, leading to the resignation of many experienced agents and revenue officers. Upon reopening, the IRS faced a backlog of mail and a reduced workforce. Consequently, new hires received minimal training, resulting in less effective tax issue resolutions.

Common Tax Issues For Individuals

Individuals commonly face the following tax issues:

- Unfiled returns: Many people neglect to file their tax returns on time.
- Underreported income: Individuals often fail to report all their income, especially when they do not receive a Form 1099.
- Inability to pay: Taxpayers frequently struggle to pay their taxes when they are due, including estimated tax payments.

Remember, it is your responsibility to report all income, regardless of whether you receive a W-2 or a Form 1099.

Reasons For Non-Payment Of Estimated Taxes

There are several reasons why people might not pay their estimated taxes:

1. Lack of knowledge: Taxpayers may not be aware of their obligation to pay estimated taxes, often due to a lack of information from their tax preparer.

2. Misallocation of funds: Some individuals may spend their money on other needs or wants instead of setting it aside for estimated taxes.
3. Changes in income: An increase in income from the previous year might lead to owing estimated taxes, but taxpayers may not realize this if they were not required to pay them the previous year.

Estimated taxes are calculated based on the total tax from the prior year. You should divide 90% of that total tax into four equal installments, which are due on April 15th, June 15th, September 15th, and January 15th of the following year.

The Consequences Of Missing Quarterly Estimated Payments

Missing one or two quarterly estimated payments is a significant issue for several reasons:

1. Large tax bills: You may owe a considerable amount of money on Tax Day (April 15th) that you might struggle to pay.

2. Underpayment penalties: Failing to pay estimated taxes throughout the year may result in an under-withholding penalty, which means you will have to pay extra fees for not meeting your estimated tax obligations.

Filing Taxes Despite Missed Estimated Payments

If you have missed some or all of your required estimated tax payments for an entire year, it is crucial to file your tax return. There are two separate penalties: one for not paying your taxes and another for failing to file. A late filing penalty can reach up to 25% of the tax due. Therefore, it is essential to file even if you haven't made your estimated payments or cannot pay your taxes when due.

Filing Taxes Versus Not Filing At All

It is better to file your tax return even if you owe money, as not filing will result in non-filing and late filing penalties. If you cannot pay your taxes, there are options available, such as installment agreements or seeking other assistance.

Filing Taxes After Missing Multiple Years

If you have not filed taxes for several years, the appropriate course of action depends on the number of years missed:

- One missed year: File the overdue return, then contact a tax attorney to help coordinate between the past and current years.
- Several missed years: Consult a tax attorney who can advise you on how many returns you need to file.

Typically, the IRS expects the current year's return and returns for the past six years. For example, for the 2022 tax year, if you haven't filed since 2010, you would need to file returns for 2016 through 2022. In most cases, the IRS is satisfied with the past seven returns. However, if a revenue officer requests an older return, you will need to file it.

CHAPTER 3

HANDLING TAX ISSUES FOR BUSINESS OWNERS

Assisting Businesses With Tax Issues

While most tax problems occur with small businesses (sole proprietors, single-member LLCs, etc.), assistance is available for all types of businesses. Common issues include failure to file payroll tax returns, unemployment returns, corporate returns, or partnership returns, all of which carry penalties. Additionally, businesses often struggle to pay their quarterly taxes when due. The majority of tax issues for businesses involve payroll tax matters.

Concerns and Consequences for Businesses Facing Tax Issues

Business owners and key decision-makers may face serious consequences when dealing with tax issues with the IRS or state authorities. Potential repercussions include:

1. Business closure: The IRS or state can shut down a business that ignores warnings or revenue officers. The IRS can obtain a court order to close the business, while the state may revoke the business license.
2. Loss of customers: Tax problems can lead to a loss of customers, especially if the IRS publicizes the notice.
3. Levies on the business: Both the IRS and the state can levy a business's bank account and empty its funds. Also, the IRS can issue a levy directly to your customers directing them to send the IRS all of what they owe you. This can

put you out of business very fast. This can result in business closure.

It is crucial to address tax issues promptly to avoid these consequences and maintain the stability and reputation of your business.

Common Business Tax Mistakes

Business owners often make mistakes when dealing with their taxes. A common error is prioritizing other bills, such as utility payments, over IRS obligations. This can lead to serious consequences, including business closure. Another typical mistake is not setting aside withheld employee taxes in a separate account to ensure timely payment of payroll taxes.

Resolving Business Tax Issues

If your business owes a substantial amount to the IRS, consider the following options:

1. Immediate action: Consult a tax attorney as soon as you receive a letter or visit from a revenue officer. They can help negotiate a 60-90

day window to organize your finances and help you develop a plan.

2. Installment agreements: Work with your tax attorney to establish an installment agreement, allowing you to pay off the debt over time. Sometimes this can be payments on a basis other than monthly payments, depending on the income stream of the company.
3. Offer in Compromise: In rare cases, the IRS may accept an Offer in Compromise for a business, though they generally prefer installment agreements.

When To Hire A Tax Attorney

It is crucial to involve a tax attorney when dealing with tax debts, particularly if a revenue officer contacts you. He can help you navigate the process and avoid common pitfalls. Additionally, attorneys can assist you in answering audit questions and ensuring you do not unintentionally incriminate yourself or provide inaccurate information. Reach out to a tax attorney as soon as you receive a letter from the IRS or become aware of a potential issue with your taxes.

CHAPTER 4

WHAT YOU NEED TO KNOW ABOUT FAILING TO PAY TAXES

Consequences Of Not Paying Taxes

Here are some possible consequences if you choose not to pay your taxes:

- Tax Liens: The IRS or the state can place a lien on anything you own in the county where it is filed. This can make it difficult to sell property and affect your credit rating.

- Tax Levies: The IRS or the state can take your money through bank levies or wage levies, depending on your situation. They can also issue levies to your customers if you are a business owner.
- Bank Levies: Your bank freezes your account for 21 days upon receiving a levy notice. If you don't resolve the issue with the IRS, the bank will send the money to the IRS. Although the levy only applies to the funds in the bank on the day the levy is received, the IRS can issue new levies regularly to catch incoming funds.
- Wage Levies: Your employer withholds a percentage of your take-home pay based on a chart provided by the IRS or the state. In South Carolina, for example, the state takes 25% of your gross income.
- Business Closure: If you own a business, the IRS can close it down due to unpaid taxes.

Tax Liens Against Individuals And Businesses

The IRS can place a lien against you or your business, affecting everything you own in the county in which the lien is recorded. Liens are generally filed for debts over $50,000, although exceptions can occur. It's crucial to seek legal assistance to resolve tax issues and possibly release the lien. For example, pursuant to the Fresh Start program, one can request that the lien be released if the debt is less than $50,000.

It's never too late to resolve tax issues:

- Consult an attorney as soon as possible to begin the process of resolving your tax debt.
- In some cases, the IRS may release a lien if specific actions are taken promptly.

Common Mistakes In Resolving Tax Issues

Individuals and businesses may make several mistakes when trying to resolve tax issues on their own:

- Ignoring IRS Letters: Some people might avoid responding to IRS notices, believing the IRS will overlook their case. However, this is not true, and inaction can result in serious consequences.
- Misunderstanding Offer in Compromise: Attempting an Offer in Compromise without

proper knowledge can lead to rejection and extend the statute of limitations for the IRS to collect the debt.

- Continuing to fail to file a return: After failing to file one year's return, many people are afraid to file the next year and thus the problem grows. Even if you do not file for a year, you should be sure to file the following year to avoid more penalties and interest.

When To Hire A Tax Attorney

Here are some key indicators for when to seek professional help:

- Unresolved Tax Debt: If you're aware of unresolved tax debt, seek legal assistance to help address the issue.
- Contact From Revenue Officer: If a revenue officer contacts you, it's essential to immediately consult with a tax attorney who can represent your interests.

CHAPTER 5

TAX RESOLUTION STRATEGIES WITH THE IRS

Effective Strategies For Resolving Tax Issues

Your attorney can help you explore several options to resolve or reduce tax issues with the IRS:

1. Offer in Compromise (OIC): A detailed calculation based on your financial situation, determining an amount to propose as a settlement to the IRS. This option allows you to

pay less than the total owed amount if you qualify.

- Payment Methods: Pay 20% of the proposed settlement amount up front, and the remaining 80% within five months after acceptance. In the alternative, you may choose to pay the proposed settlement amount in 24 monthly installments, beginning in the month in which you file the Offer.
- Rejection and Appeals: If your OIC is rejected, your attorney can evaluate whether to accept the decision or file an appeal.

2. Installment Agreement: A payment plan to pay off your tax debt over time, with various options available.
   - Streamlined Installment Agreement: Calculate the monthly payment that will pay off the debt in full within the Statute of Limitations (the period of time during which the IRS can collect the debt). In this case, the taxpayer will not have to provide any financial information to the IRS. This allows you to keep certain assets.

- Financial Analysis-Based Installment Agreement: Determine the monthly payment based on your income and allowable expenses, which might result in not paying the full amount owed before the collection statute expires.

3. Currently Not Collectible (CNC) Status: If your expenses exceed your income and you have no assets to borrow against, the IRS may suspend collection efforts for up to two years. However, the tax is still owed and interest continues to accrue.

- Periodic Review: The IRS will review your financial situation after 18 months to two years to determine if you need to begin an installment agreement or maintain CNC status.

4. Penalty Abatement: Whenever returns are not timely filed and/or taxes are not timely paid, the IRS charges penalties against the taxpayer in addition to the interest that is charged for non-payment. Each of these penalties can add up to 25% or more of the total tax. Therefore, after several years, the interest and penalties can add

up to more than the tax. The IRS never forgives interest charges but many times they will agree to waive or lower the penalties if reasonable cause is shown. This is done through a Penalty Abatement Appeal. You should always retain a good tax attorney to file this appeal for the greatest chance of success.

5. Appeals: When the IRS refuses to accept your Installment Agreement, Offer in Compromise, or other proposed resolution, you have a right to appeal that negative decision to the Appeals Division. In this way, you get a second chance to have your proposal approved. The Appeals Division revenue officers have wider latitude in accepting proposals than the collection revenue officers, so you can often get your proposed resolution accepted in appeal, even if it was initially refused.
6. The Fresh Start Program: This is a widely misunderstood program offered by the IRS. It does not mean that the IRS will forgive your taxes and let you start over. It is available for

those who owe $100,000 or less. It has two main objectives: (a) A lien will generally be released upon application and good cause shown. (b) If the taxpayer can full-pay the debt within the Statute of Limitations by making monthly payments, no financial data will be required by the IRS.

Understanding The Collection Statute Of Limitations

The IRS generally has 10 years to collect taxes from the date you filed your return. However, certain actions, such as filing bankruptcy or submitting an Offer in Compromise, can extend the statute of limitations. When the time runs out, the IRS will write off the remaining debt.

CHAPTER 6

ADDRESSING IRS CHALLENGES AND SAFEGUARDING YOUR FINANCIAL FUTURE

Qualifying For Tax Resolution Options With The IRS

While there are resolutions available for every taxpayer with delinquent taxes, not everyone can qualify for reduced payment options. For those with significant income or valuable assets, the IRS may require payment in full. However, others may qualify for an installment agreement, an Offer in Compromise, or a Currently Not Collectible status.

Attorneys And Negotiations With The IRS

Experienced tax attorneys can help with negotiations and settlements with the IRS. They understand the regulations and processes involved, allowing them to navigate the system effectively on behalf of their clients.

Timeline For Resolving Tax Debts With The IRS

The time it takes to resolve a tax debt with the IRS varies significantly depending on the complexity of the case and the efficiency of the IRS agents handling it. In general, resolving a tax debt can take anywhere from six months to two or three years, with some cases being settled in as little as 30 days. Factors such as the residual impact of Covid and the competency of IRS agents can influence the timeline.

Protecting Taxpayers From Future Tax Issues And Liabilities

To avoid future tax issues and liabilities, taxpayers should file accurate tax returns and pay their taxes on time. For most people with more than just a W-2 and standard deduction, it is advisable to hire a competent tax preparer who knows the ins and outs of tax regulations and uses reliable software to file taxes correctly.

Choosing A Tax Preparer

When selecting a tax preparer, it is important to seek recommendations from others and thoroughly evaluate their qualifications. Beware of tax preparers who promise large refunds before reviewing your financial records, as they may be scammers. In some cases, such individuals might falsely report business activities on tax returns to generate large refunds, leaving the taxpayer to deal with the consequences when the IRS discovers the discrepancy.

To protect yourself, be cautious when choosing a tax preparer and avoid those who make unrealistic promises or engage in questionable practices.

Finally, whoever you choose, you should always review your return before signing it.

What Sets Our Firm Apart in Guiding Businesses And Individuals Through Tax Problems

A competent tax attorney is crucial for resolving tax problems early on before they escalate and become more difficult to manage. Clients often come to us after receiving a call, notice, or letter from the IRS, and they are understandably concerned. Our approach involves:

1. Reassurance: We reassure clients that their tax issue is a debt, similar to a car payment – and that we can resolve it. Although the IRS has more authority than other creditors, our experience and knowledge allow us to navigate these situations effectively.
2. Honesty and Reputation: Our firm is known for its honesty and integrity. We receive many

referrals from attorneys, CPAs, and satisfied clients who trust our expertise and commitment to their cases.

3. Skilled Staff: Our well-trained staff is capable of answering questions and providing guidance, ensuring that clients don't always have to speak directly with an attorney for assistance.
4. Communication: We prioritize prompt and clear communication with our clients, responding to their calls and emails in a timely manner. Keeping clients informed and addressing their concerns is essential for building trust and maintaining a strong working relationship.
5. Strong Relationships with Tax Authorities: Our firm has an excellent reputation with the IRS and state tax agencies. This rapport is crucial, as it helps facilitate a smoother resolution process for our clients. Tax authorities know that when we propose a solution, we have put in the necessary work to ensure its viability, increasing the likelihood of approval.

Our approach to guiding businesses and individuals through tax problems sets us apart from other firms, offering clients peace of mind and confidence in our ability to resolve their issues.

INDEX

NOTES

Made in the USA
Monee, IL
05 November 2026

67387956R00029